STILL COUNTIN' MY BLESSINGS

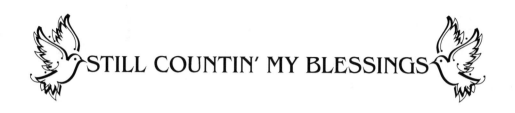
STILL COUNTIN' MY BLESSINGS

Maxine Dykes Quinton

authorHOUSE®

AuthorHouse™
1663 Liberty Drive
Bloomington, IN 47403
www.authorhouse.com
Phone: 1 (800) 839-8640

Published by AuthorHouse   12/12/2017

ISBN: 978-1-5462-1964-4 (sc)
ISBN: 978-1-5462-1963-7 (e)

Print information available on the last page.

Any people depicted in stock imagery provided by Thinkstock are models,
and such images are being used for illustrative purposes only.
Certain stock imagery © Thinkstock.

This book is printed on acid-free paper.

Because of the dynamic nature of the Internet, any web addresses or links contained in
this book may have changed since publication and may no longer be valid. The views
expressed in this work are solely those of the author and do not necessarily reflect the views
of the publisher, and the publisher hereby disclaims any responsibility for them.

Scripture taken from The Holy Bible, King James Version.

CONTENTS

DEDICATION

First and foremost, I dedicate this book to my God for all the blessings He has bestowed upon me. I thank Him for talents He has given to me. May I use them to bring honor and glory to His name.

I'm thankful for my family. I have a daughter and three sons. My second son, Steve, passed away in 2009 at the age of forty-eight. I have eight grandchildren and four great grandchildren as of November, 2017.

I dedicate this book also to my entire family:

My children Mike, Leasa and Mark
and their families
And to the memory of my son, Steve.

AFTER ALL

After all is said and done,
      I'm not bitter, I'm better,
You know why?!
      I've read God's Love Letter.

He loves me unconditionally
      whatever I say or do,
He says, "Now child,
      you belong to Me, I love you."

Even when I mess up,
      He's always there by my side,
He just corrects and
      encourages me to always abide.

Don't misunderstand,
      I'm not perfect, but I do strive,
So, one of these days,
      the gates will swing open as I arrive.

God Himself, will say,
      "Welcome home daughter of mine,
Heaven is your new home,
      you can leave all the world behind!!"

SCAR ON YOUR HEART? GOD HEALS!

If you're going through something
      that's leaving a scar on your heart,
Just give it to Jesus,
      He'll do much more than His part.

He'll apply a healing ointment
      of forgiveness and love,
In your heart you'll know
      it's straight from above.

You'll remember that scar
      but on it be sure not to dwell,
For after time passes
      you'll realize it's healed and well.

If we didn't have hurts
      and disappointments to bear,
Then we wouldn't know
      about God's love and God's care.

Even though we don't understand
      why they have to be,
We must trust that God knows best
      for you and for me.

Now, Satan will bring them to your memory,
      putting on you the blame,
But! Just tell him to "Get thee behind.
      I'm under The Blood in Jesus name!!"

WE MUST LOOK UP

We must look up
　　　for the strength we need.
His hand is always there,
　　　His children to feed.

We must be humble
　　　and listen to His voice.
We must look up
　　　and make Him our choice.

Life can be so complicated
　　　at the very least.
But, by trying,
　　　on His many truths we can feast.

Sometimes, we feel so alone
　　　and our spirit is down.
But, by looking up,
　　　that's where our strength can be found!!

IN JESUS' NAME

When I'm at a loss,
     He's always working for my gain.
When I feel downhearted,
     if I look up and pray in Jesus' name.

Then all things will work for my good
     each and every time,
'Cause my Lord sets a table
     and invites me to come and dine.

He serves me spiritual food
     that blesses and fills my soul;
You know what? This story of God's love
     is the greatest ever told.

So! When you are feeling low,
     remember He's working for your gain.
Just open up your heart to Him
     and pray in Jesus' name!!!

JUST IMAGINE

Just try to imagine!
      Strolling down that golden avenue.
Just imagine!
      Being one of God's chosen few.

To pass through the gates of pearl
      and see The Wonderful Light!
Shining on everyone
      so gloriously bright.

The walls of jasper
      and the city made of gold;
Won't it be wonderful
      for our eyes to behold?

And to walk by the river of life
      with water so crystal clear,
To pick the fruits from the tree of life
      that grows so near.

Imagine! Shaking hands
      with the apostle Paul,
And seeing the prophets
      and disciples one and all.

Yes! We can try to imagine
      but come what may,
We can never know
      such a glorious world until that day!!

THE BRANCH AND THE VINE

I'm just a little bitty branch,
      but I'm clinging to The Vine,
If I stop clinging,
      Hey! I won't be worth a dime.

I must stay connected
      in order to grow to perfection,
So, I'll keep on clinging,
      growing in the right direction.

The best and only direction is up;
      you know why?
'Cause by clinging, my destination—
      That Heavenly City in the sky!!!

FROM SHYNESS TO BOLDNESS

From a shy freckle faced little girl
      with pigtails in overalls with a bib,
So shy, she couldn't say a word
      not even to tell a fib,

But, she could talk to the animals
      that she did or did not know,
Especially to horses,
      whispering and saying, "giddy up" or "go".

But life changes everyone
      as they learn to converse and talk,
Now, that "little" girl is still a little shy
      but can talk and walk the walk,

'Cause God gave humility and boldness
      both at the same time,
She can speak out
      and write encouraging words that rhyme.

Today, she is bolder
      and not hardly as shy,
And she thanks God,
      'cause He's the reason why!!!

A HUG FROM HEAVEN

Ever felt a hug
        straight from God above?
Ever felt His still small
        voice of love?

Ever been enveloped
        by His love so complete?
Recognizing His touch
        as being ever so sweet?

When you suffered a loss
        you've yet to understand,
Just reach up,
        He'll take hold of your hand.

He'll sustain your hurt
        by giving you a heavenly hug;
At the same time,
        He'll give your heart a special tug.

For He knows every disappointment
       you've been through.
He knows the forlorn feeling
       inside of you.

He'll lift you up
       when you feel so let down.
He'll give you a smile of hope
       to replace your frown.

He'll give you courage
       to hold your head high,
And let you know
       that He'll always be nigh.

So, if you ever feel sad, lonely,
       let down or blue,
Just wait, He'll give you a hug
       and carry you through!!!

A DIRECT LINE

We have a direct line to God's Heavenly Throne,
  No put on hold,
  No call waiting,
  No fifteen options,
  No leaving a message,
  And no call back number,
'cause Jesus always answers, taking care of His own.

Yes! Our Lord always answers and says,
  "What is it my child?
    Whatever it is, I'll be with you every mile!"

FROM HOBBLING TO JUMPING

My feet and legs get numb and tingly;
  but I'm still hobbling along,
Hobbling, hobbling
  while singing my victory song,
Hobbling, hobbling on my way
  to that land called Heavens Glory,
But! On my arrival,
  I'll be jumping for joy telling my own story.

LET'S EXERCISE OUR SMILING MUSCLES

Have love in your heart and a smile on your face,
Then you'll be happy every single mile in this life's race.

'Cause a big old pretty smile,
Will help you to run every mile.

A smile is just a frown turned upside down you see,
But a true smile only comes from the heart of you and me.

A smile can speak when no words are spoken,
And a smile can help mend a heart that is broken!

So! Let's keep on exercising our smiling muscles!

TAKE TIME FOR SIMPLE THINGS

How do we spend our time each day?
Why not turn that 'box' off and say,

I'm gonna set on the porch or under a tree,
And know that God will surely meet with me.

And spend 'simple' time listening for His call,
And seeing the beauty He's provided for all.

Why not enjoy the quietness that is all around?
You know what? If we do, it lifts up and not down.

We don't need to be too busy for the simple things;
So, let's slow down, take time each day till our heart sings!

PSALM 17:8

Keep me as the apple of your eye,
        hide me under the shadow of thy wings,
Give me strength, fill me with heavenly love
        until my heart sings.

Walk with me, talk with me,
        give me courage to stand for You wherever I go.
Lord, help me be an example of Your Way
        and determined to defeat the foe.

Help me praise Your holy name
        in whatever my life brings to me,
And reach out to others encouraging them
        to turn to You on bended knee.

Thank You Lord for all You do for me and my family
        each and every day,
And thank You Lord for salvation,
        the only hope for all is all I can say!

THE IDEAL DIET

Wanna go on a diet
    that will give you perfect health?
Well, a Bread and Water diet
    will also give you untold wealth.

I'm referring to a diet of Bread of Life
    and Living Water for the Soul,
With this unending diet
    you'll be in shape for that City of Gold.

So, let's feast each day on this diet
    from His Holy Word,
And we'll have that glorified body
    to live forever with our Lord!

GOT YOUR AMUNITION WITH YOU?!

We are in a battle,
      so we need ammunition to fight the enemy for sure.
The only way to fight is to be armed and ready
      with His Word so we can endure.

Let's read, study and hide It
      in our hearts every single day.
Then we'll be ready to shoot
      and knock old Satan out of the way.

He has to back up
      when The Word is thrown in his face.
So, let's put on our armor,
      pick up our sword and win life's race!!

THE WEB OF SIN

Let's not lose our focus
    and get caught in the web of sin.
The spider, being Satan weaving
    an evil design to catch us in.

As a spider weaves a beautiful design,
    it has a purpose that's deceiving.
That spider waits to devour its prey
    from the web it's been weaving.

Just like the spider, Satan causes sin
    to look beautiful to our eyes.
So! Let's pray to not fall prey
    to Satan's web of tricks and lies!!

BLOOD TYPES

We each have a blood type,
      such as AB, O positive, O negative and A,
But Jesus' blood is pure
      for a transfusion any old day.

Yes! His purifies us
      from head to toe when applied,
He shed His for you and me
      when on the cross He died,

So, let's thank Him for The Blood
      that covers all sin,
'Cause without It,
      the victories of life we could not win!!

EMPTY TO FULL

Empty your being
     of any hate, grudge and pride,
And He will put His Great Love
     and Forgiveness on the inside.

Get rid of hurts and disappointments;
     just give them to Him,
And He will give you joy and peace
     to replace them.

Then take His love, joy and peace
     with you every single day,
Then you can overcome
     any obstacle along The Way!!

SMILE TO A FROWN

Let's put an ugly frown
  on old Satan's face,
By showing him
  who's gonna win this life's race.

When he comes around us,
  talking to our mind,
Let's quote scripture
  and tell him to get thee behind.

He's a sly old fox,
  he watches us and knows when to speak,
But, with God's help,
  we can be strong, not weak.

Hey! Let's put old Satan
  way, way down,
By changing his smirky smile
  to a permanent frown.

So, we must stay ready
  and alert to his tactics of wrong,
By looking up in prayer
  and singing our victory song!!

YOU'RE INVITED

Want to have a 'PITY PARTY',
        or go to a 'HALLELUJAH HOEDOWN'?
The choice is yours
        but the 'Hoedown's where good things are found.

The 'Pity Party',
        it just causes you to feel let down,
But a 'Hallelujah Hoedown' is where
        spiritual strength can be found.

Your spirit is lifted
        and your soul is surely blessed,
Because the Holy Ghost is there,
        He's the Special Invited Guest.

So, without further adieu,
        let's have someone give us that piano sound,
Let's be in one mind and accord
        and have a spiritual 'HALLELUJAH HOEDOWN'!!!

THE SWORD
(God's Holy Word)

We have a daily battle,
      but THE SWORD is our weapon each and every day,
So, we must know about this weapon,
      it's truth, it's strength
      and how to use it along this way,

But, to know this weapon, we must
      read it, study it
      and hide it in our hearts,
Then our Lord will give us wisdom
      to be able to fend off Satan's darts.

The Holy Word, it's like a two-edged sword
      dividing right from wrong,
If we apply ourselves
      then in the bye and bye
      we will sing THE VICTORY SONG!!

OUR DESIRES—HIS WILL

God can make all the arrangements
  to grant the desires of our heart
  if it's in His will.
All we need do is ask,
  remain faithful to live His Way,
  believe and just stand still.

He knows just what to do
  in all situations
  to allow our desires to be.
Then when they happen,
  we can forever praise Him
  for all He does for you and me.

But if they're not in his will,
  we must be willing
  for it not to be.
Because He knows best
  what's best for you
  and for me!!

CHARTERED FLIGHT

I've never flown on an airplane in this world
      and I don't want to.
But, I'm booked on a chartered flight to Glory Land,
      how about you?
I'm just plain old chicken
      when my feet are very far off the ground.
But I'll have no fear as I board
      that special flight that's Heaven bound.
So, if you're not booked on that flight,
      add your name to The Book of Life.
Then on that great day,
      together we can leave this world of trouble and strife!!

FROM HERE TO THERE

Lord, as I close my eyes in death,
      may I be filled with Your great peace.
Then my spiritual eyes shall awaken in Your presence
      to that marriage supper feast.
May I leave behind to my family the example of Your peace
      of living right and not wrong.
May my voice be as an angel in that heavenly choir
      singing my victory song!!

LUKE 23:34

"Father, forgive them
    for they know not what they do."
Touch our hearts to forgive
    and be more like You.

Lord, don't allow us to feel,
    "I will get even".
Lord, cause us to look up
    and be more like Steven.

No matter what
    this road of life may bring,
Put within our hearts
    a special song to sing.

May that song tell others
    of a God-given victory.
And may we gain that victory
    on bended knee.

Lord, we are human,
    but if on Your word we rely,
We know that sufficient grace
    You will supply.

So, Lord, as we go from day to day,
    help us to look up.
And help us to empty our soul
    and present to You an empty cup!!

BREAD AND WATER

Are you hungry?
     What about a special
     bread and water diet from above?
Our Lord will feed you
     Bread of Life and Living Water
     plus heavenly love,
Now, John tells us about
     The True Bread from Heaven
     and Living Water for our soul,
So, let's all go on this diet
     and it will take us
     to that City of Gold!!

COME AND DINE

From my porch I see Robins, Cardinals, Doves
     and little birds I know not their kind.
As my birdseed is spread all around,
     they always "come and dine".

Hey! Isn't that just like our Lord?
     He spreads a special table every day.
But, we have to "come and dine"
     to gain grace and strength along this way!!

SO, LET'S COME AND DINE!!

MY LONGINGS

I'm longing for Heaven
      to see my Savior's face on that great day.
I'm longing to hear
      "Well done my daughter," He will say.

I'm longing to see those gates of pearl
      and that city filled with His love.
I'm longing to see my loving Momma
      and other family and friends in that city above.

I'm longing to see Mrs. Quinton (my Naomi)
      for she was a Jewel here below.
Yes, I'm longing to join all in Heaven;
      I really miss them so.

And I pray I will see my children and their families
      in Heaven's Gloryland,
And I will, if they all serve Him
      and hold on to His great big hand!!

NOW HERE WE ARE

Now here we are again
     in the house of the Lord.
We've come to worship Him
     and study His Word, the Sword.

We should be reverent and respectful
     and not go to sleep,
'Cause, He may come while we're napping;
     then we'd weep.

For, He's coming so quickly,
     we can't say, "wait for me,"
We gotta be spiritually dressed
     and spiritually ready, don't you see?

Our soul must be pure and clean
     and without spot or blemish,
'Cause this race is about over;
     we're nearing the line of finish.

So, put on your spiritual armor
     and open your eyes to the light.
If you look real close at the Eastern sky;
     His coming is clearly in sight!!

MOUNTAINS AND VALLEYS

We all like the mountain top experiences of our lives,
  we all know,
But it's in the many valleys of testing
  where we really grow.

Just like a farm,
  the bottom land grows the crops the best,
Because there's richer soil and a water supply,
  don't you guess?

SO, just like our valleys, the richness of God's Word
  and His Living Water helps us to grow,
So, let's not complain about valleys,
  'cause they help us yield Good fruit, don't you know?

God's Word says to be thankful
  for all things of life that come our way.
Sometimes that's really hard to do,
  but we must accept and please Him every single day!!

VALUABLE ANTIQUES

I'm just an old antique,
      becoming more valuable every day.
I'm just old antique,
      the Lord has brought me a long, long way.

I'm just an old antique,
      but I keep on walking for my Lord.
I'm just an old antique,
      to stop keeping on, I just can't afford.

If you're an old antique,
      let's join hands and walk together,
Then one of these days,
      we'll be taken upward, lighter than a feather.

So, as we old valuable antiques
      keep walking this road of life,
Remember, our Lord said He would be with us
      through any strife.

As I said, we're becoming more valuable every day,
      but not in dollars and cents;
But in power from above,
      to tell 'old slew foot' to get thee hence!!

MY LORD, MY BIBLE AND ME

Here I sit this morning,
     my Lord, my Bible and me,
Meditating on His Word
     and how He set me free.

As I read His Word,
     it speaks of His Love so very true,
When you read It,
     I hope It speaks words of encouragement to you.

I pray you'll read His Word daily
     and in His great love abide,
Then we'll both know
     that He's always by our side.

As we reach up,
     He'll always be there waiting to reach down,
Giving us strength daily
     to wear a smile and not a frown!!

HUMOR, RUMOR, CARE, SHARE

I thank God
      for my high sense of humor.
Being happy in the Lord is real
      and not just a rumor.
When we look up and not down,
      knowing we're in His care.
Then we can pass it on to someone;
      His great love we must share!!

A PRAYER

Lord, help me walk upright,
And be pleasing in Your sight.
Help me to stay on my spiritual diet,
Keep me strong to stand and fight.

Focus my mind to do what's right,
Lead me to always walk in the light
And hold Your hand with all my might.
May I be aware of Your love day and night.

Then by and by, I'll dwell in that city ever so bright!!

31

ARE YOU DOWN AND OUT?

When you're down and out
     and don't feel like going on,
Just open up your heart
     and sing a happy song.

Look up, get in God's Word
     for strength to go another mile,
Then you'll be able to tackle anything
     with a great big smile!!

DOORPOSTS

Do we have The Blood applied
     over the doorposts of our hearts?
If so, we're equipped to fend off
     all of Satan's darts.

But, if not, we can talk to our Lord
     and He will apply.
Then, we'll be safe from harm
     and join Him in the 'Sweet By and By'!!!

BREAD—DRINK—SWEETENIN'

When we eat a good hot biscuit or a good piece of hot cornbread,
    maybe with jelly or honey—What a treat! What a treat!
And then drink something good to wash it down
    —That's a combination that is so hard to beat!

When the 'bread' and the 'liquid' get together in our stomach;
    What happens?
    They expand, causing us to feel full and robust.
And for a short time, we are filled to the brim
    and feel we must take a nap—Oh! We must!!

Too much of a good thing for our physical being
    is not always the best, you see.
But, let's use another example, that really,
    we can't over-indulge in if we digest it, you and me.

This other example also concerns 'bread' and 'liquid',
    being a good combination of two.
The 'bread' is Jesus Christ, the 'bread of life',
    and the 'liquid' is the 'living water',
    springing up like a well in me and you.

Just as physical bread needs 'sweetness' to taste better;
    Its taste is improved so very much,
So does the 'bread of life' and the 'living water' need sweetenin',
    that being 'The Holy Spirit's' touch.

We all agree, bread and sweetenin' and a drink are good together;
    We know without being told.
But, the treat that can't be beat
    is His Three In One for the soul!!

SPIRITUAL UMBRELLA

Let down your spiritual umbrella
    and let it rain, rain, rain.
Let down your umbrella,
    look to the sky for spiritual gain.

Just look up and feel
    those heavenly raindrops on your face.
You'll be refreshed in your soul
    as you run this important race.

God said He will pour out
    so many blessings we cannot contain.
So, let's let down our umbrella
    and get ready for that latter rain.

Surely He's getting ready
    to take a ride on a cloud from Glory.
He's gonna finish the last episode
    of that old, old story.

Yes, let down your spiritual umbrella,
    get ready for that trumpet sound.
You don't want to stay here;
    so, let's all stay Heaven bound!!

SAUL TO A PAUL

Have we had The Damascus Road experience,
      changing us from a Saul to a Paul?
If so, we must walk, talk, look,
      be different and stand tall.

'Cause we can't hold on to our old man habits
      and make it in.
That's what Damascus Road is all about
      —to keep us away from sin.

So, to anyone who has not walked
      The Damascus Road, may I suggest,
Take a walk on that road
      and get acquainted with The Best!!!

EVEN IF

Let's keep looking up
  and looking ahead.
Let's walk with our Lord
  as daily we are fed.

Even if food at Walmart, Save-a-Lot
  and Kroger gets too high to buy;
As in the days of old, our God can rain down
  manna from the sky.

One definition of manna is that it's a wafer
  that tastes similar to honey.
So, if necessary, our Lord can feed us all
  without any money.

So, let's keep looking up and ahead,
  knowing that He will provide,
If in His Way we always
  truly trust and abide!!!

A PRAYER WE COULD ALL PRAY

Lord, help me make a difference
       as I walk along this way.
May I be a source of encouragement
       to someone every single day.

When I see someone struggling
       or know they're feeling low,
May I help them to look upward
       to know You love them so.

Lord, as I travel this journey,
       give me strength to travel on.
Hold my hand, help me look upward
       and remember I'm never alone.

Thank You, Lord for all You've brought me through
       in this earthly life.
May I look forward to that Heavenly home
       where there is no strife.

Lord, I want my family to go with me
       to that beautiful Glory Land.
So, Lord, reach down and shake them every one
       to take hold of Your hand!!!

GOD AND GOLIATH

Just pretend your problem is named Goliath
        and let God throw the stone.
Yes, take hold of faith's hand
        and go to battle, but not alone.

Let God fight the battle
        and you'll have the victory.
Yes, God is always ready
        to help you and me.

We just need to back up
        and let Him go ahead.
He'll give us the victory,
        that's what He said.

When victory comes, we can say,
        "look what God did for me!"
It's really very simple,
        Just let Him do the fighting, don't you see?!!!

TARES

Am I, or are you,
      what His Holy Word calls a tare?
Or, are we able to look at others
      and say, "I really care?"

Perhaps we should check ourselves
      to see just how we really stand.
If not, seek forgiveness
      and hold on to His mighty hand.

Then, only with His help,
      we can make correction.
By doing so, we can go up
      in that final resurrection!!!

DEFEAT THE THIEF

Lord, help me defeat the thief
     by totally depending on You.
Put a hedge around me and my family
     that Satan can't break through.

Make it so thick and thorny
     that he'll get caught in his own trap.
Oh Lord! Give me a spiritual strength
     that I may stand in the gap.

While laying my family at Your feet
     each and every day,
Praying that they will truly turn to You
     and walk in Your Way.

So, again I ask, help me defeat the thief
     by depending on You.
Give me strength to keep on keeping on
     whatever You do!!!

HE'S ALWAYS NEAR

He's reaching out His hands saying,
      "give Me all your burdens and cares."
He's reaching out His hands
      for all our troubles He always shares.

Oh! If we would only give
      all our concerns to Him.
He loves us so much that
      He will always take care of them.

His hands are big enough
      to provide every need we have here below,
And He will always reach down and protect us
      from that ever-present foe.

Yes, He'll fight that foe for us
      no matter what,
If we trust Him to be
      the best friend we've got!!!

RAINDROPS

I see raindrops on the tree branches
      just outside my front door.
They're just hanging there being beautiful,
      causing my thoughts to soar.

As I drink my cup of tea;
      seems God put them there just for me.
He's like that you know;
      creating things lovely for our eyes to see.

Soon the sun wipes away the branches' tears
      and shines to light the day.
God's order is perfect,
      if we but open our spiritual eyes and see His way!!

WE GOTTA BE READY

Oh, we gotta be ready
      for those fiery darts,
Satan's gonna shoot
      and aim straight for our hearts.

He'll keep on shooting
      as fast as he can,
But God's shield of faith
      will help us to stand.

And just when we think
      we've got it made once more,
He shoots again,
      trying to even the score.

But, he knows he loses
      the battle in the end,
Yes, God's shield of faith
      will always outdo his sin!!!

WHAT A DAY

What a day it's gonna be
    — when He takes us home.
What a day it's gonna be
    —we'll nevermore roam alone.

What a day it's gonna be
    —when we meet our Savior in the sky.
What a day it's gonna be
    —we'll forever praise Him in the by and by.

What a day it's gonna be
    —will you all be with me there?
What a day it's gonna be
    —I hope all knows how much I care.

What a day it's gonna be
    —walking those streets of gold.
What a day it's gonna be
    —I want us to hear the rest of the story
        that's never been told!!!

WOW!!

If you are someone who thinks
      you are alone most of the time,
Just look up and around
      and you will see and won't be blind.

God is with you every moment of the day;
      just send up a word of prayer,
'Cause He said He would never leave you;
      He would always be there.

And if you find yourself
      feeling sorry for yourself and blue,
Just tell old Satan to "get thee behind"
      and your day will become new.

Yes, just start counting
      your blessings up to now,
Your heart will rejoice
      and may you say with feeling, "WOW!!"

FROM MY HEART

From my heart and my mind
      I write what God gives me.
I'm happy to write encouraging words
      from me to you, don't you see?

'Cause if they help you on your way,
      then they help me too.
Encouraging words always help someone
      to look up and not be blue!!

HELP NOT HINDER

Let's not be miserable comforters
      to anyone in their grief.
Let's be encouragers to them,
      helping them gain relief.

Let's be their friend,
      helping them look up to the Lord,
'Cause that's where victory is found
      according to His Word, The Sword!!

FORGIVE TO BE FORGIVEN

Let's live this life of ours
     to forgive so we can be forgiven,
'Cause if we don't,
     we may fail to please our Lord while we be a livin'.

Every day He blesses us with our needs,
     perhaps even the desires of our hearts,
And also gives us power to fend off
     every single one of Satan's darts.

Things that God has brought us through,
     we should not dwell on the past,
Let's just look to Him for strength
     and we'll make it to Heaven at last!!

THANK YOU LORD

Thank You Lord
>for Who You are and for Your Way.
Thank You Lord for strength
>You give to me each and every day.

Thank You Lord for my family;
>they're precious in my heart.
Thank You Lord for Your love,
>help me to always do my part.

Thank You Lord for provisions;
>You know just what I need.
Thank You Lord for courage
>to go about scattering good seed.

Thank You Lord for Your promises
>to all who will come to You in prayer.
Thank You Lord for Your Returning
>to take us to our Heavenly home up There!!!

BOLD HUMILITY

Lord, give me boldness to step forward
     and humility to step back to just the right place.
Then, Lord, use me to Thy glory in many ways
     while I'm running this race.

For, if I'm bold enough to talk
     and just humble enough to be meek,
Then, I can wait;
     You will give me words of wisdom to speak.

So, use me Lord,
     in many various ways to whatever extent,
Then, with help from Your Spirit,
     I will be happy and content!!

LIFE

As we go through life,
    it takes from us things that are real.
But, if we accept,
    God will replace; He will heal.

As a child, we look to Mom and Dad
    to make everything work out right.
They can heal bumps and bruises
    and chase away fears in the night.

As we become young ladies and young men,
    we listen to all well-meaning advice.
And if we heed those words,
    there's nothing wrong with the word nice.

As we go a little farther in life,
    we come to a fork in the road.
Do we go our own direction
    or do we ask someone to share our load?

As we make our own well-meaning decisions,
    we find we can make mistakes.
Then we lean on God
    to help us turn loose of what life takes.

As life touches our home,
      turning it inside out and upside down,
We can look to Him;
      He will give us a smile to replace our frown.

As we allow Him to touch our heart
      and the very depths of our soul,
He replaces hurt with heavenly hope
      as we give Him complete control.

As we give Him complete control,
      we can see life in a different light.
We walk on in spite of our loss
      and our faith makes it alright.

As we walk through valleys low
      and soar mountains high,
We know He walks there with us;
      His spirit is ever nigh.

So, whatever life takes from us
      as this way we go along,
We can just simply look to Him;
      He will put within our hearts a lovely song!!

Maxine Dykes Quinton

THE 'SON' AND THE 'SUN'!!

As the SUN is peeping through the clouds
      at the start of the day,
The SON always peeps through our clouds
      all along this way.

So, if clouds are overshadowing your situation,
      no need to fret,
'Cause He's always with us,
      how much more blessed can we get?

Let's just praise His name
      for each and everything,
For He is our Savior, Lord
      and our Eternal King!!

A MOTHER'S PLEA

A loving mother always wants the best
      for her children as they come along,
And she knows the most important thing
      she can teach them is right from wrong.

So, as they grow she encourages them
      to learn and do their best,
And to follow Jesus through life
      and He will do the rest.

Some minds Momma on this road of life
      but some surely rebel;
But, Momma keeps on pleading
      'cause she wants to keep them out of hell.

So, we mommas keep on keeping on
      making our loving plea,
'Cause no matter their age,
      we love our babies as we pray on bended knee.

So, you mommas, let's keep on praying
      and making A MOTHER'S PLEA;
Then, perhaps some sweet day in Heaven
      our precious babies we'll see!!

READ, STUDY AND HIDE

Have we taken up
     THE SWORD today?
It's needful to defeat Satan
     along this Way.

So, let's Read, Study and Hide IT
     in our hearts,
Then, we can tell Satan,
     "It is written" when he shoots his darts.

Let's Read and learn
     what It says each and every day,
It's our weapon to fight old Satan,
     come what may.

Let's Study and ask our Lord
     for wisdom from above,
He'll fill our being with understanding
     and with much love.

Let's Hide His Word in our hearts
     in case our Bibles are taken away,
'Cause state and federal governments
     could do that just any day.

God will always protect us,
     but we must apply ourselves and make a start;
So, let's READ, STUDY and HIDE IT
     each and every day, that's our part!!

ETERNAL VACATION

I'm gonna take a long vacation
   very soon past the Milky White Way,
I'm not coming back,
   gonna stay longer than forever and a day.

My mansion is being made ready for me
   with my name over the door.
I made my reservation years ago,
   gonna live there forever more.

Gonna go through those pearly white gates
   into that City of Gold.
My eyes will be on Jesus,
   then all of Heaven's beauty I'll behold.

My Lord is preparing a supper for His Own,
   the Marriage Supper of The Lamb;
I pray my family will be with me there
   as we praise The Great I Am.

I pray you've made your reservation,
   joining me on that flight to Gloryland,
And if so, we can all sing together
   in that Heavenly Angel Band.

If not, I encourage you
   to get on your knees and be born again,
Then you'll have a reservation
   to fly out of this world of sin.

So, let's all be sure we're ready for that eternal vacation, AMEN!!!

IN MY DISTRESS

In my distress
      I called upon The Lord.
He said, for comfort,
      pick up The Sword.

Arm yourself with Words
      and feelings of love,
Then the strength you need,
      will come down from Above!!!

JUST TRUST HIM

If you are of age
      and know what to do in your heart,
Or if you're very young
      and maybe don't understand in part.

Just trust Jesus;
      He'll help you to have courage to take a stand,
All you need do with your life
      is reach up and take His hand!!!

THE OLD AND THE NEW

Off with the old man
  and on with the new,
That's what God does
  for me and you.

When we open our hearts door,
  He walks right in,
And applies His Redeeming Blood,
  covering our sin.

Yes, off with the old
  and on with the new,
That's what He does
  for me and you!!!

IT'S ONLY TEMPORARY

This life on earth is only temporary,
  so let's strive to make the best of it
  as we go along.
But, there's coming a time that's permanent
  when we'll live forever,
  singing our Heavenly Victory song.

We'll crown Him Lord of Lords
  and King of Kings
  on that Great Day.
So, let's make up our minds
  to determine to Live in The Way,
  His Way!!!

TAKE ACTION, GET BUSY

Look up
  and not down,
Wear a smile
  and not a frown.

Get busy,
  go out and about;
Tell the Good News
  with no doubt.

Walk The Straight and Narrow
  every day.
Pray that others will follow
  along the way.

Listen for that still, small
  Voice of Love;
Then, abundant blessings
  will flow down from Above!!!

MUMS NOT THE WORD

When referring to The Word,
      our word should not be 'Mum'.
In that respect, we don't need
      an idle mind or an idle tongue.

Reading and studying His Word
      fills us and hides It in our hearts.
Satan wants us to be 'Mum',
      but when we speak It, he departs.

So, let's not let 'Mum' be our word
      when it comes to The Word,
Let's take time to read It and speak It,
      making sure It's heard.

Remember, 'MUM's NOT THE WORD!!!

DO WE LOVE OUR LORD ENOUGH?!

Why don't we love Him
      like we used to do?
How come we treat Him
      like a worn-out shoe?

He blesses us but gets too little praise
      from me and you,
So, why don't we love Him
      like we used to do?

For thirty-three years,
      He did many miracles, not a few,
Then died on The Cross;
      He did it all for me and you.

He loved all He met,
      even His enemies too;
So, why don't we love Him
      like we used to do?

Perhaps we're more takers than givers
      to you know who,
We take all He gives with no thanks,
      that's a bad point of view.

So, why don't we love Him
      like we used to do?
For sure, we need an attitude change
      that's brand new.

Then without a doubt we'll all love Him
      much, much more than we used to do!!!

ANOTHER THANK YOU LORD

Thank You Lord for another year
      of provision and protection for me.
Thank You Lord for Your mercy and grace
      and for Your Salvation that's free.

Thank You Lord for the safety of my family
      as they go about each day.
Thank You Lord for each breath I breathe
      and for guiding me along The Way.

Thank You Lord for my little corner of the world
      I have here below.
Thank You Lord for loving me
      and for strength to fight that ever present foe.

Thank You Lord, I know You'll always be with me
      as I walk the rest of The Way.
Thank You Lord for that City of Gold where I'll join that chorus
      and sing Victory's song some sweet day!!!

OH LORD

Oh Lord, may we be aware
  that Your coming is very nigh,
That You are coming to take us
  to that home on high.

Please pour out conviction on our lost family
  and friends here below,
Touch their lives in such a way
  to shake'm to wake'm to know.

They must turn to You
  before it's everlastingly too late.
Please don't let Satan deceive them
  and forever seal their fate.

Yes, Lord may we be aware
  and tell everywhere we go,
That You're coming soon
  in such a way that all will know!!!

IT'S IN THE BOOK

In school we had text books
      for reading, writing and arithmetic.
We had to read and study those books
      for the learning to stick.

But we have the greatest text book of all
      or will ever be;
It's a long love letter,
      written especially to you and to me,

IT'S IN THE BOOK!!!

Will we enroll in the school of knowledge,
      repentance and belief?
If we enroll and apply ourselves,
      there will be a great relief.

'Cause by repenting and believing,
      we'll be rewarded with a BA degree,
And that's the best degree
      for mortals like you and me.

IT'S IN THE BOOK!!!

Now, that Born Again degree
      will give us joy in our heart and soul,
And cover us with grace,
      give us hope and help us to be bold.

If we keep on reading and studying,
      blessings will keep coming down.
With joy in our hearts,
      we'll defeat the devil with a smile over a frown.

IT'S IN THE BOOK!!!

Yes, as we cultivate our spiritual gardens,
      me and you,
Our lives will bear fruit
      as told in Galations 5—22.

Love, Joy, Peace~~~IT'S IN THE BOOK!!!
Longsuffering, Gentleness, Goodness~~~IT'S IN THE BOOK!!!
Faith, Meekness, Temperance~~~IT'S IN THE BOOK!!!

Whatever we need to know
      about living the Christ like way;
This love letter has all the answers
      if we'll apply them every day.

For It's the Bread of Life and Living Water
      for our soul's health,
And by taking It at It's Word,
      we will receive an untold wealth.

IT'S IN THE BOOK!!!

NO MANSION DOWN HERE

I want no mansion down here,
        just want that one in the sky.
It'll be custom made by my Lord
        in that city on high.

No mistaking it,
        for my name will be over the door.
It'll be decorated in Heavenly style
        and I'll live there forever more.

Won't have rent to pay, no groceries to buy
        or bills addressed to me,
For in that golden city on high
        everything is provided for free!!!

BUY, SELL OR TRADE THIS
SALVATION—NO WAY!!!

I didn't and couldn't BUY IT,
      'cause it wasn't for sale.
Christ already paid for it at the Cross;
      He paid my bail.

When I called on His name,
      His precious blood covered me.
No! No! I couldn't BUY IT,
      because It was free.

Now I'm not gonna SELL IT
      to anybody of this world below,
'Cause if I did, then I wouldn't have
      anything to fight that old foe.

I know that foe is out to get me and you
      every single night and day,
So, "Get thee behind me Satan"
      is what I must be ready to say.

And to TRADE God's Way for something else
      is simply out of the question;
To TRADE for this world's way
      would only bring me sin's infection.

Don't you know His Way
      is the best choice of life any old day,
So, I'm not SELLING or TRADING This Salvation,
      that's all I got to say!!!

HEAVEN

Hey! I'm looking forward to Heaven,
  how about you?
Just think for a minute
  of what we won't have to do.

Won't have to go to the filling station
  to buy gasoline,
No Walmart, Kroger or Save-a Lot
  for meat that's lean.

No rent or house or car payments
  to pay at all,
No heat and air-conditioning bills
  and not even one phone call.

No dishes to wash, no sweeper to run,
  and Whew! No grass to mow.
You know, Heaven sounds greater and greater to me,
  don't you know?

No health problems
       or painful hip, shoulder or ankle joints out of place;
Why we won't have a single one
       of these ills to face.

No doctor appointments to keep
       or hospital visits to the ER,
'Cause our health will be perfect
       in that heavenly place afar.

But, just in case God
       has some chores for us to do;
We'll delight in every one
       in that place beyond the blue.

So, we've got a great future
       to look forward to.
All will be perfect in Gloryland
       for me and for you!!!

JONAH

Old Jonah wouldn't go fishing for The Lord
      in Ninevah's direction;
So, The Lord allowed a storm to blow
      to make needed correction.

Since Jonah disobeyed
      and in a sense told God to wait;
He wouldn't go fishing in Ninevah,
      so, Jonah became bait.

Can't you just imagine
      being caught in that fish's belly;
In yucky surroundings
      about to be digested to resemble jelly?

But, Jonah changed his mind
      after being vomited on the shore;
Old Jonah wasn't stubborn
      and disobedient any more.

Yes, just in time
      Jonah became obedient and willing,
To go where God said,
      therefore, God's will fulfilling.

Jonah was stubborn and rebellious,
      was gonna do things his way,
Kinda like us sometimes,
      but with God's mercy and forgiveness,
      we'll make it home someday!!!

KEEPING MY JOY

I'm gonna keep my JOY
      even if it hairlips the devil;
Just ain't gonna give up
      and stoop to his level.

I've got ever so much
      to be happy and joyful about;
Jesus in my heart, peace in my soul
      —that deserves a shout!

So, if you want JOY, put Jesus first,
      Others second and yourself third,
Then quote scripture to Satan;
      he'll scram after hearing The Word!!!

SLIM OR FAT AND FLOURSHING?

Marie Osmond has a diet
    where you lose weight and become oh so slim,
But God has a diet of bread and water
    that makes you fat and flourishing in Him.

Now, Marie's diet costs a pretty penny
    I'm sure for you and me,
But, God's diet is simply His Word
    and for sure it's oh so free.

Don't have to order online
    and pay a big price ahead of time;
Just simply open His Book,
    digest His Words, then walk The Line.

Now, our physical health is important;
    we should treat our body as a temple.
But, our spiritual health is much more important;
    its upkeep is very simple.

Eat It, Digest It
    and Wear It ever so well,
And It will surely
    keep us out of Hell!!!

PERFECT BOOKKEEPER

God is a perfect bookkeeper;
      He records every word we say each and every day,
It all goes into His Book of Life;
      the life we live all along this gospel way.

So, we must be careful what we speak
      and, also what we think;
If we don't, into a world of sin
      and confusion we will sink.

So, let's try to have a good record
      for our Lord to keep account of,
Then, every day He will send His sweet love
      like on the wings of a Dove!!!

MEMORIES

Memories, memories hanging on my wall
        and lingering in my mind;
They are forever here in my memory,
        but I must leave them behind.

No matter my feelings,
        my Lord is always by my side,
And I can always rest assured
        that He will always abide.

Memories, memories in my memory bank,
        some are good, some are bad,
Some surely bring a smile,
        then some will only make me sad.

The good ones I remember
        making me happy and never blue.
As for the bad ones,
        the Lord has surely brought me through.

So, I must stop and look ahead,
        remembering what's in store for me;
I'm gonna leave this old world
        and a Beautiful Heaven I'm gonna see!!!

ASK, BELIEVING

As I sat on my porch
      one warm morning facing the East,
I fed my birds and was just sitting there
      also having a feast.

A feast on God's creations—
      the sun, the blue sky, flowers and the trees.
The air was very warm; in my mind,
      I asked the Lord for a little cool breeze.

I just sat there meditating on my family
      and how blessed I had been,
Then! Surrounded by a cool breeze,
      I said, "Thank You Lord, on You I can depend."

You know, He'll even send a cool breeze,
      if we but ask, believing.
And if our faith is strong enough,
      whatever we ask for, we'll be receiving!!!

Maxine Dykes Quinton

HIS HOLY WORD, OUR SWORD

Do we know the truth
     of the gospel of our LORD?
His HOLY WORD—
     It's our weapon, it's our SWORD.

But! We must read and study It
     to know how to use It,
To fight our battles every day;
     we can't give up and quit.

Reading It every day and adding prayer
     gives strength we need,
Then we'll be strong every day
     in every word and every deed!!!

ANOTHER DAY ON MY PORCH

As another day comes to an end,
    Thank You Lord for carrying me once more,
And Lord I trust You will carry me
    'til I reach that Golden Shore.

But Lord, I want my family
    to be with me over there also,
So please reach down and shake them
    to realize and know.

That You are the only way
    that leads to that Heavenly city above.
Please Lord save my household
    with Your great Heavenly love.

So, Lord as this day ends
    and perhaps another is on the way,
Keep on carrying me
    and may I be pleasing to You each and every day!!!

Maxine Dykes Quinton

LOOKING BACK, LOOKING AHEAD

Looking Back, we can see all
      that He's brought us through.
Looking Back, He woke us up each day
      with provisions for me and you.

Looking Back, perhaps we lost a loved one;
      He was there all the time.
Looking Back, in His sanctuary,
      we were welcome to come and dine.

Looking Ahead, He will always take us
      through whatever comes our way.
Looking Ahead, He will provide all our needs
      each and every day.

Looking Ahead, if we suffer disappointment,
      He'll always be by our side.
Looking Ahead, this new year, we should make sure
      in His Love we abide!!

~ HAPPY NEW YEAR!!! ~

LET'S #1

Let's make every day be like another Christmas day,
        but only the giving part.
Let's show spiritual love to others,
        sincerely from the heart.

Let's give encouragement and friendship
        to someone each and every day.
Let's be sincere in every good deed
        all along the way.

Then we'll have peace
        and be blessed beyond compare.
Our Lord in Heaven will be pleased
        from His Throne up There!!!

LET'S #2

Let's all pray the Old Year out
        and pray the New Year in at midnight;
Ask the Lord to bless our families
        to open their eyes and see The Light.

May we all thank The Lord
        for all our blessings this past year,
And make a resolution to walk
        in such a way to keep Him ever near!!!

HE'S ON HIS WAY

He's on His way, He's on His way;
  He could arrive at any hour,
When it happens,
  all will know His Almighty Power.

So, let's be sure we're ready
  and watching each and every day,
Then we can go back with Him
  past The Milky White Way.

Gonna be a flight that's filled
  with His peace and great love,
'Cause our destination is sure—
  that Heavenly City up above!!!

WHY ARE WE HERE?!!

Are we here for the right reason
      or just for show—me and you?
Or because we for sure need to,
      want to and have to?

We must live for the right reason,
      to honor and worship our Lord above,
And to fellowship with one another
      and show much Christian love.

So, perhaps we need to look in a mirror
      and check that person's heart,
To see if it's full of love
      and willing to always do its part.

As for me, I'm gonna be here, if possible,
      'cause there's nothing I'd rather do;
So, I hope you feel the same way,
      then, we can all be happy and never blue!!!

HE IS THE ANSWER

Do you have a problem?
　　　Do you have a need?
Just talk to Jesus,
　　　then follow His lead.

He'll take you through the fire,
　　　He'll take you through the flood,
'Cause long ago He went to Calvary;
　　　He took the stripes and shed His blood.

So, whatever problem that you have,
　　　He's the answer to one and all,
Remember, He's always available
　　　to answer your call!!!

- HE IS THE ANSWER!!! -

HE'S MY STRENGTH

Lord, give me strength, give me strength,
      strength for the day,
Yes, strength Lord,
      as I daily walk this way.

Forgive my weaknesses as I follow You
      all the days of my life,
I need Your strength to take me
      through whatever strife.

Thank You Lord in advance
      for all You will do.
Thank You Lord;
      I can lean on no one but You!

THANK YOU LORD!!!

PERHAPS

When nothing seems to be happening,
      perhaps something is;
Perhaps God is softening a heart,
      for we know the best timing is His.

When a loved one is running from God,
      it breaks our hearts in two,
But God has His Master Plan;
      He knows just what to do.

He's the Master Potter
      that can soften that heart to repent;
So, when nothing seems to be happening,
      perhaps something is being Heaven sent!!!

MOUTH, MIND AND HEART

Lord, please guard my thoughts
  and the words that I say.
Also, Lord, post an angel
  at the door of my heart every single day.

Help me check myself
  in all that I do everywhere I go,
Then, Lord, I'll be strong in You
  and always able to fight the foe.

Yes, guard my mind, my mouth,
  but most of all my heart,
'Cause what's in my mind and my mouth
  comes from the heart; the main part!!!

IN LOVE WITH JESUS

I'm in love with Jesus
    and He's in love with me;
He died on the Cross of Calvary
    to set me free.

I'm in love with Jesus
    and He's in love with me;
I met Him one day
    down on bended knee.

Are you in love with Jesus?
    I know He's in love with you;
If you're not,
    open up your heart to become brand new!!!

THANKFUL OR UPSET?

We've got more to be thankful for
      than we have to be upset about;
With so many blessings,
      we really should stand and shout!

We seem to take a lot of things for granted
      as we go along.
We really should look to The Cross;
      He'll surely give us a song.

Singing a little song from the heart
      helps give us strength for each day;
Even "Jesus Loves Me" would help us
      walk and talk His Way
         all along this way!!!

READY OR NOT

Ready or not we're going down or up
      on that great day,
When Gabriel blows that horn,
      it'll be too late to pray.

So, please don't wait to make up your mind
      to get in The Way.
Hey! Your eternal destiny is your choice;
      what more can I say?

Except that God loves you
      and He's waiting with open arms today,
So, make up your mind,
      get down on your knees and pray, pray, pray!!!

I'M LONGING, ARE YOU?

I'm seeing now
     those beautiful gates of pearl,
That will open wide
     as I leave this world.

Then my eyes will behold
     that city foursquare;
Oh! My Lord,
     I'm getting eager to go there.

I'm looking forward
     to those streets of gold,
And to meet
     all those saints of old.

But, most of all
     to see my Savior and Lord.
Then I'll worship Him forever
     and receive my reward!!!

JUST RIGHT!

There's a pot of gold at the end of the rainbow,
        so I've been told,
But I'm going to a city of rainbow colors
        and streets of pure gold.

The Word says we cannot imagine
        what it will be like,
But with our God as Master Designer,
        it will be just right!!!

THANK YOU LORD

Thank You Lord for Your Will,
        Your Way
                and Your Word;
All three are the very best ever heard.

If we read His Word
        to know His Will
                then walk in His Way,
Then we'll be victorious soldiers each and every day!!!

THE SWORD, PICK IT UP!!

We can't fight if It's on the coffee table,
      shelf or, God forbid! on the floor,
So, let's pick It up, learn to use It
      more and more, as never before.

If we'll read and study to learn
      all we need to know about living right,
Then we'll be able to use 'the Sword'
      to outdo the enemy day and night!!!

A REAL GOOD DEAL

I traded my sin for His forgiveness
      and got the best end of the deal, don't you see?
He put my sin in a sea,
      then I received His forgiveness and felt so free.

My guile, iniquity and transgressions
      are covered by The Blood—He did His part,
So, now I have much joy, love
      and His sweet peace within my heart!!!

ONLY HIS WAY

When He calls our name,
     will we be alert and ready to go?
When we reach The Pearly Gates,
     will He say "yes" or will He say "no"?

Oh!! People, let's look in the mirror
     and keep that person straight,
Then we'll have no worry
     about going through those Pearly Gates.

If we keep ourselves straight,
     our light will shine out to others,
Then we can surely walk the narrow road
     with our sisters and brothers.

If we keep on walking and talking
     only His Way,
Then we'll see The Great I AM
     some sweet and glorious day!!!

TURN LOOSE, HOLD ON, LOOK UP

Turn loose of all sin
      and things that confound.
Hold on to faith, hope and love
      and be heaven bound.

Don't we all want a white robe
      and a Heavenly crown?
Just thinking about it
      should put us on shouting ground!

So! Look up, look up,
      He's surely on His way.
That trumpet sound
      could be just any day!

GET BUSY

When we're down and out
      and don't feel like going on,
Let's open up our hearts
      and simply sing a happy song.

Let's look up; get in God's Word
      for strength to go another mile,
Then we'll be able to tackle anything
      with a great big smile!!!

SITTING ON MY PORCH

In the quietness of the morning
      I feel restful in my soul.
I feel my Lord so near;
      His presence to always unfold.

Sometimes it seems no one is awake
      but the birds in the sky,
But I know my Lord is with me;
      His presence is ever nigh!!!

THE MASTER IN THE UPPER ROOM

From tears to joy
  is sometimes a lonely road to travel,
If we aren't careful,
  we can allow ourselves to unravel.

But if we look up to Him
  and ask for help from above,
He's sure to hear and send His love
  like on the wings of a dove.

If we'll just wait,
  tears of joy will fill our hearts to overflow.
Yes, our Lord will always send an answer,
  because He loves us so.

So, if you are crying tears
  of disappointment and gloom,
Just open your heart
  and talk to The Master in The Upper Room!!!

PEACE

The peace in my life
     is like manna from above,
Fills my heart to overflowing
     with peace like a dove.

Gives me strength
     for each and every day,
Helps me keep walking
     and talking His Way.

I thank my Lord for this peace
     living within my heart;
I know He'll keep on giving,
     as long as I do my part.

If your peace gets weak
     and turned upside down,
Just look to Him;
     He'll turn it right side up and turn it around!!!

LOOK TO THE CROSS

Look to the Cross
      for all that you need.
Just humble your heart;
      your soul He will feed.

Remember, He gave His all
      for you and for me;
He bled and died on the Cross
      that we could go free.

He came to earth
      that all mankind could have life;
Yes, He's always with us
      through any strife.

But, we must trust Him
      and believe in our heart;
So, let's LOOK TO THE CROSS
      and always do our part!!!

HURTS

All kinds of hurts come our way;
      we can't seem to understand.
But, one thing for sure
      our Lord is always reaching down His hand.

He knows ahead of time
      our hearts will break from on the inside,
But, when we trust Him,
      He will always be our guide.

After the hurt is soothed,
      life will go on and we'll know for sure,
That our God will always be there,
      helping us to endure.

So, in the midst of these storms,
      He sends peace from on High,
'Cause, just as sure as birds fly,
      our Lord will always be nigh!!!

REVIVE US

Revive us oh Lord, revive us oh Lord;
      may we awake from our sleep,
May our eyes be opened to reality
      and humbly weep.

Revive us oh Lord;
      may we get busy doing more for You,
And be determined to please You
      in all we say and do.

Revive us oh Lord,
      may we fall on our knees in repentant prayer,
Then, as our life ends,
      we'll be with You in that city foursquare!!!

A BLESSING IN DISGUISE

Sometimes a hurt comes along
     and tears our lives upside down,
Then the Lord brings us through it
     and peace is found.

As result, a blessing shows up
     causing the hurt to temporarily depart,
Then, we know God had a reason
     for that hurt that touched our heart.

So, we keep on going
     no matter what comes our way,
'Cause we trust Him to strengthen us
     every single day.

We don't forget the hurt,
     but we don't dwell on it and ask the 'whys',
But, after all is said and done,
     sometimes a hurt is a blessing in disguise!!!

DON'T BE ASHAMED TO CRY

It does a body good to cry
  if we let our hearts be our guide;
Crying releases emotions of happiness
  or sadness from the inside.

Sometimes thinking of a loved one of the past
  brings tears to our eyes,
But thinking of what they meant to us
  is where a blessing lies.

So, let's not be ashamed to let
  tears run down our cheek,
Our Lord will give strength to be strong
  and not at all weak!!!

WAITING FOR JESUS

I'm a waiting for Jesus
    to split the Eastern sky.
I'm ready and a waiting;
    that time is ever nigh.

This world is a great mess;
    we must all agree;
Let's strive to walk upright,
    staying on bended knee.

Whether bowed in an humble position
    or bowed in our heart,
We can all work and pray
    therefore, doing our part.

I'm still waiting;
    are you ready and waiting for Gloryland?
Yes, let's watch the Eastern sky
    and hold onto His hand!!!

HEAVEN OR HELL??!!!

Heaven or Hell
     —which will it be?
There's only two choices
     for you and me.

We die and return to dust
     from which we came;
So! Please, won't you choose Heaven
     in Jesus' name.

If you choose Hell,
     you'll forever burn with no end,
And forever you'll be wishing
     you had forsaken sin.

I've made my reservation
     for my mansion in the sky.
So! Please make your reservation;
     His coming is so very nigh!!!

MY HOMEPLACE IN THE SKY

I grew up without a home place
        without knowing why.
But! Now! I have a Heavenly Home Place
        way up in the sky.

And I'm on my way
        to live up there forever more;
There's a mansion there
        with my new name over the door.

With golden streets
        and a crystal river that runs nearby,
No street lights,
        'cause Jesus is the Light in that city on High.

Along with The Father and The Holy Ghost,
        they make up The Trinity;
So, I'm looking forward to seeing my home place
        built especially for me!!!

A PRAYER

Lord, as I kneel in my heart
      or on bended knee,
Help me stay right here
      'til I hear from Thee.

Touch me with Your spirit
      and let me feel You near;
Keep me still so I can know
      You are whispering in my ear.

Cause my heart to soften
      and my eyes to shed some tears;
Remind me to know I'm blessed
      and push away any fears.

Keep me safe tonight,
      looking forward to another day;
Strengthen my faith for the future,
      come what may!!!

ROCK AND ROLL

My foot's on The Rock
        and my name's on The Roll,
'Cause one day Jesus came
        and He saved my soul.

He covered me with His precious blood
        and made me pure;
That's how all these many years
        I've been able to endure.

Yes, endure hurts and disappointments
        all along the way,
So, I'm gonna keep my foot on The Rock,
        come what may.

Hey!! You got your foot on The Rock
        and on The Roll?!
Well! There's only one way;
        that's through Jesus Christ;
        HE'LL SAVE YOUR SOUL!!

    SO! GET ON THE ROCK AND ON THE ROLL!!!

GOD'S LITTLE ME

Hey! I'm a little girl or little boy
        and I'm so sweet,
And I know Jesus loves me
        in a way that's oh so neat.

He loves me when I'm good
        and also when I'm a little bad,
And He loves me when I'm happy
        and also when I'm sad.

Now, I'm learning about Him
        and how to be good every day.
I'm learning the Bible characters
        and how they learned The Way.

So, just be patient with me
        as I grow and grow;
Love me and teach me
        all the things I need to know.

Things I learn will all stay
        even though I'm LITTLE ME,
Then, when I'm grown,
        I'll remember what I need from A to Z.

Please, ask Jesus to keep me safe
        from dangers I cannot see.
Here's my hand;
        lead LITTLE ME to HIM—that's the key!!!

HAPPY MEAL

You know, McDonalds has a complete HAPPY MEAL for one
      plus a toy,
But! Christ fed a group of 5000 with one child's meal
      plus leftovers and joy.

He has a HAPPY MEAL for us every day,
      if we get in line and wait;
By having that HAPPY MEAL every day,
      we can surely go through HEAVEN'S GATE!!!

A GIFT

A gift wrapped in love, tied with a golden cord of humility
      with silver threads of grace,
Sent from Heaven to earth to a lowly manger,
      to rise in victory for this human race.

Our Lord's birth, death and resurrection
      was given from God's heart of love,
To save us, take us home to Glory,
      to reign with Him Above!!!

I'M LEAVING, WON'T BE LOOKING BACK

When I leave here,
      I'm going to a better place;
I want my memory to be
      one of truth and grace.

As I take my last breath,
      I want to see my Savior's face;
I want to see the love in His eyes
      that just won't erase.

I want Him to lead me across that river
      to that Heavenly shore;
I won't be looking back
      for I'll live there forever more.

I'm gonna eat a different fruit each month
      and drink from a crystal stream.
My mansion will be decorated in Heavenly style;
      it won't be a dream.

As I walk those golden streets,
      I'll join my family and others I have known;
We'll be singing praises to our Lord and King,
      to Him alone.

All will be joy and happiness
      as we sing our victory song in a Heavenly key;
All will be perfection,
      for God Himself has it all prepared for you and me!!!

THE CROSS AND THE BLOOD

You can trust in The Cross;
      you can trust in The Blood,
Anytime the enemy comes at you
      like a flood.

But, if you lay down your trust
      even for a minute,
Satan will surely use
      each and every second in it.

He'll lead you for sure
      the wrong way,
'Cause it's his desire
      to lead us astray.

So, hold on to your Cross
      and claim The Blood,
And you can ride out any storm
      and ford any flood!!!

SALTY AND SHINY

If we don't be salty,
        we will lose our savor,
So, let's be salty on earth
        and not lose God's favor.

If we don't shine,
        we cannot block out the darkness,
So, let's shine His Light
        and be a Heavenly success.

Now, let's be salty and shiny for Him
        as we run life's race,
Then, all the joys of Heaven will be ours
        as we look upon His face!!!

SUNRISE

Lord, you gave me a beautiful sunrise this morning
　　　using Your spiritual ink;
It spread across the sky with
　　　pinkest orange and orangey pink.

It was such a lovely site
　　　against Your canvas of blue;
All the artists of the world
　　　cannot paint such as You.

They must mix and mix
　　　to come up with the right shade,
But You just speak
　　　and that sunrise is perfectly made.

Then You spread it across the sky
　　　just so a mortal like me,
Can behold the beauty of the morning
　　　and be blessed with eyes to see!!!

ANOTHER PRAYER

Help me Lord to walk upright,
And be pleasing in Your site.

Help me lean on You day and night
And tell old Satan to go fly a kite.

'Cause You are helping me to win this fight;
Every day You always feed me a spiritual diet.

And You surely guide my feet to walk in The Light,
So, I'm gonna keep pressing with all my might.

AND then some sweet day I'll take my Heavenly flight!
REPEAT—I'll take my Heavenly flight!!!

SPIDER'S WEB—SATAN'S WEB

As a fly gets caught in that web
      that a spider spins,
No way the fly can escape;
      it's caught—the spider wins.

But, if we humans get caught in Satan's web,
      you and me,
We have an awesome power
      that surely sets us free.

So, to avoid Satan's web
      and always be aware,
Let's take on humility
      and stay in constant prayer!!!

A PRAYER

Lord, may I always be
   pleasing in Your sight,
May my walk each day
   as I go, be upright.

I need You every day to shun the wrong
   and hold on to the right,
I love You Lord;
   help me to walk each day in The Light.

I desire to hear Your still small voice,
   so, help me be quiet.
Thank You Lord for all You do;
   may I listen with all my might.

For I know You're coming back;
   it may be morning, noon or night,
So, give me strength for the journey;
   yes, strength to win this fight!!!

THANK YOU LORD

Thank You Lord,
       Thank You Lord for always being near,
In times of joy or
       when we're shedding a tear.

You always give us strength
       to make it through,
So, we just need to keep on
       trusting You.

Sometimes we bring things on ourselves
       by making a wrong choice,
But, He's always with us
       hoping we'll listen to His voice.

So, if we take time to delight,
       commit and trust as in Psalm 37.
Then wait for His will;
       we're certain to make it to God's Heaven!!!

BEFORE AND AFTER

If we were called and had to go to battle
        in the U.S Military,
If we went with no headgear, shoes or weapon,
        it would be plain old scary.

We would prepare before battle,
        not wait till the enemy had us in his sight.
We would have our helmet, shoes, weapon,
        ready to fight.

So-o-o! Don't you think we need to be spiritually ready
        each and every day?
'Cause old slewfoot is bound to come at us
        to keep us from THE WAY.

Yes! Each day we need to get up
        and put on the whole armor to take us through,
So, let's praise Him, read His Word, pray
        and reach out to others, me and you.

Being prepared before the battle,
        not waiting till the enemy has us in his sight,
After we prepare, then God will give us
        all the strength we need to win this fight!!!

VICTORY

I've got Victory over every trial
        that has come my way.
I've got Victory;
        I'm happy in The Lord each and every day.

You might ask me How?
        I'm gonna smile and say,
"Through my Lord Jesus Christ,
        when at His feet my burdens I lay!!!"

SWORD OF TRUTH

Do we know the Truth
        of The Gospel of our Lord?
You know, It's our weapon
        —His Holy Word.

But! We must read Its instructions
        as how to use It,
To fight our battles every day;
        we can't give up and quit.

By reading It every day and adding prayer,
        we gain the strength we need.
Then we'll be strengthened every day,
        in every word and every deed!!!

LORD, HOLD ME

Lord, hold me in your arms
      when I cry tears of GLADNESS;
Also, when hurt and disappointment brings
      tears of SADNESS.

Tears in the happy times
      when the sun is shining bright,
And in sad times
      when the sun seems to be out of sight.

Happy times like holding my babies
      the first time and watching them grow,
And sad times when they hurt
      or chose to listen to the ever-present foe.

So, Lord, please hold me
      when I cry,
And soothe all my hurts
      from on High!!!

      THANK YOU, LORD
          FOR HOLDING ME
              WHEN I CRY!!!

THANKS

Thank You Lord for blessings;
      thank You for another day.
Thank You for always being near,
      leading in The Way.

I don't know what I would do
      if I did not have You,
But I know You're always with me
      in everything I do.

Thanks for my family
      that has helped make life complete.
Thanks Lord;
      You're a friend that just can't be beat!!!

THAT CITY OF PERFECTION

I'm going to that City of Perfection;
      there'll be no sorrow, no troubles or pain.
I'll know as I am known,
      happy forever and have a brand new name.

I'm going to that City of Perfection;
      I'll be rejoicing and see my Lord face to face.
He'll say, "well done my daughter,
      enter in, you've finished life's race."

I'm going to that City of Perfection;
      I'll be jumping for joy as I cross the finish line.
My Momma, my Naomi, perhaps my Steve and others
      waiting for me to come and dine.

Are you ready to go to that City of Perfection
      when it comes time for your departure?
Hope so! Let's all look forward to that city,
      whether by the grave or through The Rapture!!!

MY EARLY MORN

I saw dew on the grass
     sparkling like diamonds in my early morn.
As I beheld its' beauty,
     I felt so thankful to have been born.

And able to see God's beautiful sun
     rising in the Eastern sky.
As it warmed my face,
     I said, "Thank You Lord for being ever so nigh."

Then I saw my doves and other birds
     fly down for their morning meal.
You see, I had already scattered seeds
     for them with heart felt zeal.

Sometimes they're waiting on the electric lines,
     waiting just for me,
'Cause they've learned I put out seeds
     And, of course they're free.

While I'm sitting there,
     I sing made up songs about the serenity and quiet,
And about my Lord and Savior
     serving me a spiritual diet.

Then I take in the morning's beauty,
     I sing more songs of praise,
So, that's how I start each morning
     with my God all seven days!!!

A QUESTION—WHAT'S YOUR ANSWER?

Are you a Christian?
> Have you been born again?
Have you repented
> and been forgiven of your sin?

If not, just repent
> and ask Him to come in.
He'll fill your heart with love
> where sin has been.

Then read and study His Word
> to show yourself approved.
Then, no matter what Satan does,
> you can't be spiritually moved!!

Maxine Dykes Quinton

FOLLOW HIS LEAD

He'll be with us through this life
     and forever more.
If we follow, He'll lead us
     to that heavenly shore.

So let's learn to follow His lead,
     walking His Way.
Then, we'll all be together in heaven
     some sweet day!!

GATHERING OF THE SAINTS

Gathering of the Saints—
     what a glorious time!
Hopefully, all of your family
     and all of mine.

If so, we will all be together
     in heaven above.
Yes, what a time we're gonna have
     in God's City of Love!!

OUR HANDS IN HIS HAND

Let's hold on to that great big hand
      that's reaching down,
'Cause that's where help and strength
      can be found.

And keep right on lookin' up
      for He will surely overfill our cup
With so much faith, hope and love
      and all good things from above.

So let's hold on to His hand
      for dear life.
Then, one day we'll have no more fear
      and no more strife!!

WATER

Water, liquid water,
     we need for our physical health.
Water, living water,
     we need for our spiritual wealth.

Lack of liquid water
     can make us so very weak.
Lack of living water
     makes us soul-sick and less meek.

So, let's go to the fountain of living water
     for our soul's salvation.
Then, we'll be ready on that great day
     of losing our gravitation!!

GOING FOR THE GOLD

We hear about 'The Golden Years'
      as we grow old.
But, if we're walking His Way,
      we're heading for 'The Gold'!

The Golden City, of course,
      with golden streets to walk upon.
And meeting the Saints of old,
      like Abraham, Paul and even John.

But, most of all, seeing
      our precious Lord and Savior, face to face.
So, let's not be upset about 'Golden Years',
      just keep on running life's race!!

IN A TIZZY?! GET BUSY!

Where would we be without forgiveness
      and mercy through prayer?
We would have no knowledge
      of how to make it up there.

We would be wandering around
      with no purpose for our life.
Thank God, we have both,
      plus His grace to cover all strife.

He gives us so much,
      but are we striving to live His Way?
We must read and study His Word
      to keep striving each and every day.

If we pick up the Bible and study it,
      it will not gather any dust.
Yes, we gotta pick it up,
      study it every day—that's an absolute must.

So, I encourage you to pick it up
      and get spiritually busy.
Then, we can stand against old Satan
      and not be in a tizzy!

BUT, GOD SEES ALL

Some would say
        of you and me,
They do nothing
        that I can see.

But, God sees all,
        knowing our heart as it be.
So, what counts
        is what God sees in you and me.

To bear fruit, it can be prayer
        from the heart or on bended knee.
Prayer is part of the fertilizer
        that grows fruit in you and me.

Even when people don't approve
        of me and you,
We know that God is our judge
        in all that we do.

Maxine Dykes Quinton

ALL AT THE SAME TIME

Our Lord knows our every thought
     and He knows our every need, yours and mine
But, what's so amazing—
     He knows all about us, all at the same time.

Millions and trillions of us on this earth
     should depend on Him for our every need.
And for every situation we face,
     we should follow His lead.

Folks, we have an amazing God in heaven
     that loves us with perfect love.
And He'll keep on loving us
     as He leads us to that city above!!

HAPPY BIRTHDAY
(to the sweetheart of my church, August 2017)

There's a little lady named Sister Vesta
      —she's special to all she meets.
With her meek and quiet spirit,
      she wins the heart of all she greets.

She sings us a song without words on paper
      and shows us God's love.
And for sure, some sweet day,
      she'll sing in that heavenly choir above.

So let's wish her a 97th Happy Birthday
      and many many more.
Then, by and by, we'll all meet
      on Heaven's bright shore!!

Printed in the United States
By Bookmasters